D1215891

The Pied Piper

The Pied Piper

by
Adrian Mitchell

Oberon Books

London • England

First published in 1988 by Oberon Books Limited
521 Caledonian Road, London N7 9RH
Tel: 071 607 3637/Fax: 071 607 3629
Reprinted in 1991 and 1994

ISBN 1870259 09 2

This play is dedicated
to the memory of my loving parents,
Jock and Kathleen Mitchell.

The story

Long ago, in the days to come, Hamelin was a small town with a large market on the edge of the River Weser. During the day the town was cheerful enough. But as darkness fell each night, the streets and alleys and drainpipes and cellars were invaded by an army of horrible, hairy rats.

Rats!
They fought the dogs, and killed the cats,
And bit the babies in the cradles,
And ate the cheeses out of the vats,
And licked the soup from the cook's own ladles.
Rats!

One dawn around evening, a stranger arrived in the town. Everybody thought he was the Mystery Tramp from the Valley of Nowhere. But really he was the Pied Piper, a magical musician famous for ridding towns of pests and parasites. He travelled in disguise because he was exhausted by such pest controlling work. He wanted to retire to a nearby mountain called the Koppelburg.

The Pied Piper, in his disguise, was treated roughly by the town's two policemen, Boggle and Goggle. They threw him in the River Weser for playing his pipe without a licence. Crawling out of the water, the Piper tried to find a bed in a rubbish cart. He was settling down on what seemed to be a huge heap of hair, when the heap began to move and he found he had snuggled down to snooze on a pile of giant rats. It was midnight and the giant rats began to tear Hamelin apart.

Next morning, down the sunny River Weser drifted a small blue boat. In it sat a young girl with a bad leg. She was called Toffee Jenkins. She landed near the marketplace, where she met some of the people who sold goods in Hamelin. She met Cosima Beamer who ran a junk stall. She met old Doctor Mungadory who sold medicines for everything. She met Arianalla Skiller from the toy shop. And Nutter Mausenheimer the miller and baker. But Toffee had no money, so she could buy nothing.

Suddenly the Town Band struck up and the Saveloys arrived. The Saveloys were very important people in Hamelin. Dennis Saveloy was the Mayor of the Town, Lady Lucy Saveloy was the Mayoress and also headmistress of a school and their son, the Honourable Egbert Saveloy, was the greedy and spoiled owner of the most powerful water-pistol in Hamelin.

The Saveloy family visited every stall in the market, trying to get necklaces, toy robots and food for nothing, with the help of Boggle and Goggle, who frightened the stallholders. Finally the Saveloys left the market with their arms full of free gifts, leaving behind a crowd of shopkeepers angry that the Mayor had done nothing about the rat problem.

Back at the Town Hall, Toffee Jenkins, with a new job as maid of all work to the Saveloys, was being bossed and bullied by the hungry Mayor and his family. They feasted their faces till they were interrupted by the people of Hamelin, calling for action against the rats. Just then a stranger came knocking at the door and suddenly the Saveloys were face to face with the Pied Piper, no longer in disguise, but ready and willing to rid the town of rats.

"How much do you charge?" asked the Mayor. "Fifty quid cash, is that fair?" asked the Piper. "Fifty – listen, if you can get the rats out of Hamelin, I'll pay you one thousand golden pounds," said the Mayor. And they shook hands on that and it was a deal and the Saveloys went off to bed and the Piper began to dance a spell with his swirling feet and play a spell with his twirling pipe and the moon came out through the grimy old clouds and the notes of the pipe trickled through the air and all the rats in the sewers of Hamelin pricked up their ears and listened and raised up their muzzles and sniffed. For the tune which the Piper played was a magic tune. And it fooled the rats into believing that the moon was made of cheese and that the moonlit river was melted cheese. And the rats followed the Piper to the riverside and, one by one, they dived into the river, and drowned to death most happily in the cheesey waters.

Next day the people of Hamelin celebrated. The Mayoress paraded all the schoolchildren from her school, the Lady Lucy Saveloy's Remarkable Academy For Children of Respectable Folk, in the dark cloaks of their school uniform. The Mayor tried to take all the credit for ridding the town of rats. When the Piper appeared and asked for the one thousand golden pounds which had been agreed, the Mayor only laughed and offered him fifty. The Piper, who was very short of money, complained and sang a song about a robot to show everybody that the Mayor was a cheat. But the grown-ups of Hamelin, knowing that they would have to pay more taxes if the Piper was to receive fair payment, decided to support the Mayor. Only the children of Hamelin, including Egbert and Toffee, thought the Piper should have his thousand pounds.

The Mayor ordered Boggle and Goggle to throw the Piper and Toffee in the rubbish cart, and there they were left. And it was there that the Piper explained to Toffee how he understood the whistling language of rats and how his magical pipe could speak that squeaking language. They were deciding to settle down in the cart for a good old sulk when the children of Hamelin arrived to cheer them up. The Piper played for them and the children's dull cloaks became transformed into the brightest patchwork patterns in the world.

The Piper told the children he would lead them on a journey to Koppelburg Mountain, and when he played his pipe, they were happy to follow him, dancing and clapping their hands.

But there were difficulties on the way. First the children had to cross the Shivering Bridge of Dilvergibbon, a flimsy, high-up, wooden bridge above a gorge – where the river down below looks like a silver ribbon. The Piper warned them that they mustn't look down or their heads would turn around – so they all managed to cross in safety, except Egbert. But his head was soon untwisted by the Piper.

From that dread bridge they travelled to the Bottomless Swamp of Ombroglio. And there they saw a monster ahead of them. Everyone was terrified – except Egbert, who was crazy about monsters. He recognised the creature as the Rampant Umbrage, a hairy monster with uncountable hands. The Umbrage was so pleased to be recognised that it showed them how to pass through the swamp and decided to come along with them to the mountain.

The Piper, Toffee, Egbert, the Rampant Umbrage and the children came next to the Freezing Forest of Forafter. Soon it seemed that they would all be frozen to death. But they found and unfroze, through blowing, an Iced Knight in armour. She cut up some wood which lit itself and warmed them. Then the Piper explained to everyone that they were going to a country where there would be no time, no money, no prisons and no war, a country where everyone would share and nobody would cry.

Soon it was time to go to the mountain, but Toffee, because of her bad leg, could not keep up. The mountain opened with a terrible roar, and into the mountain ran Egbert, the Rampant Umbrage, the Iced Knight, the children and finally the Piper. The mountain began to close, but just before it did, the Piper left his pipe on the ground outside.

Toffee arrived just as the mountain closed. Toffee cried out for the Piper but there was no reply.

Then the parents of the children of Hamelin asked her if they would ever get their children back. She told them no, but perhaps they could see their children in the mountain. She told them their children were very happy, living in a good land of adventures with the Piper. But the grown-ups wouldn't believe that she could see into the mountain and became angry.

When the parents of Hamelin had gone away, Toffee found the magical pipe on the ground. She realised the Piper must have left it for her. Then she saw words on the pipe which told her that the pipe was for her. She, Toffee Jenkins, realised that she was to be the new Pied Piper. So she began to play the pipe and the sound was beautiful and as she played the pipe and walked away from the mountain towards new adventures a shooting star flew across the sky. And that was the end of the beginning.

ADRIAN MITCHELL

The Pied Piper by Adrian Mitchell, from the poem by Robert Browning, was devised and directed by Alan Cohen with music by Dominic Muldowney.

The 1986 production, opened at the Olivier Theatre on 11 November 1986 and played in repertory in the Olivier and Lyttleton Theatres until 17 February 1987. The 1987 production opened at the Olivier Theatre on 4 November 1987 and played in repertory in the Olivier and Lyttleton Theatres until 24 March 1988.

The cast of the 1986 production was as follows, in order of appearance:

Cosima Beamer, *who keeps a sweet stall*	Deborah Leighton
Doctor Mungadory, *a learned seller of potions*	John Darrell
Arianalla Skiller, *who runs a toy stall*	Sarah Prince
Nutter Mausenheimer, *a miller and baker*	Mike Hayward
Twessa Twangalang, *who runs a junk and antique stall*	Yvonne Gidden
Boko Bandy, *a wandering Australian magician*	Richard O'Callaghan
Boggle, *a heavy security person*	Graham Sinclair
Goggle, *another of the same*	Sammy Johnson
Baron Dennis Saveloy, *Mayor of Hamelin*	Shaun Curry
Lady Lucy Saveloy, *Mayoress and Principal of her own private school*	Nicola Blackman
The Honourable Egbert Saveloy, *their only son*	Bill Moody
Bobby 'Gravy' Browning, *cub reporter on the Hamelin Herald*	Elaine Lordan
Toffee Jenkins, *a young girl with a bad leg*	Wendy Morgan
King Rat	Richard Platt
The Pied Piper, a stranger	Sylvester McCoy
The Rodents	Deborah Leighton
	Elaine Lordan
	Sarah Prince
The Massed Rats, *a swarm of rats*	The Children
Captain 'Salty' Flowerdew, *Skipper of the Merry Maisonette*	Richard Platt
Pupils at the Mayoress's school	The Children
The Rampant Umbrage	Mike Hayward
The Iced Knight	Deborah Leighton

Musicians: Robert Lockhart (MD/keyboards), Anthony Aldridge (electric violin), Julia Findon (trumpet), Michael Gregory (percussion), David Roach (lyricon, Oberheim Xpander, saxophone), David Stewart (bass trombone).

The cast of the 1987 production was as follows:

The Pied Piper, *a stranger*	Sylvester McCoy
Toffee Jenkins, *a young girl with a bad leg*	Diane Bull
Baron Dennis Saveloy, *Mayor of Hamelin*	Philip McGough
Lady Lucy Saveloy, *Mayoress and Principal of her own private school*	Patsy Rowlands
The Honourable Egbert Saveloy, *their only son*	Bill Moody
King Rat	Brian Hibbard
Nutter Mausenheimer, *a miller and baker*	Bruce Purchase
Cosima Beamer, *who keeps an antique stall and a sweet stall*	Doreen Webster
Doctor Thelonius Mungadory, *a learned seller of potions*	Allister Bain
Arianalla Skiller, *who runs a toy stall*	Mary Askham
Boggle, *a heavy security person*	Ewart James Walters
Goggle, *another of the same*	Jimmy Chisholm
Lamplighters	Bruce Purchase
	Allister Bain
The Rodents	Mary Askham
	Doreen Webster
The Massed Rats, *a swarm of rats*	The Children
The Rampant Umbrage	Brian Hibbard
The Iced Knight	Mary Askham
Children of Hamelin	The Children

Musicians: Robert Lockhart (MD/keyboards), Julia Findon (trumpet), Michael Gregory (percussion), David Roach (electronic wind instruments/saxophone), David Stewart (bass trombone), Paul Maguire (assistant MD).

The children appearing in *The Pied Piper* are from the following ILEA primary schools: Addison, Bonner, Bridishe, Canonbury, Childeric, Christ Church, Columbia, Colville, Deptford Park, Dog Kennel Hill, Drayton Park, Dulwich Hamlet, Gayhurst, Grasmere, Grinling Gibbons, Hollydale, Kenmont, Lauriston, Lucas Vale, New End, St. Francis, St. John's and St. Clement's, Sir Thomas Abney, Stebon and Streatham Wells, and from the KIDS UK Theatre Group.

Settings, Roger Glossop; Costumes, Sally Gardner; Movement, David Toguri; Lighting, Paul McLeish; Staff Director, Sarah Ream; Sound, Paul Groothuis; Music in Schools, Robina Nicolson; Movement in Schools, Jennie Buckman; Production Manager (Olivier), Michael Cass Jones; Production Manager (Lyttelton), Rodger Hulley; Stage Manager, Elizabeth Markham; Music computer synthesis, Ian Cross, Walter Fabeck.

Children in the cast

They play a very essential part in the story. Some of their major tasks on stage in the show are listed below:

ACT ONE

They sing in the opening chorus.
As members of the massed Rats, they are enchanted by the Piper, take part in the singing of 'Gorgonzola Moon' and drown happily in the river.

ACT TWO

They appear as the down-trodden pupils of Lady Saveloy's school in long gowns, singing their 'School Song'.
They join in the 'Rusty Robot' chorus in order to take the side of the Piper against the Baron and his allies.
They dance and sing in the Patchwork Rap. In this scene their cloaks are reversed and they join the Piper's expedition to the Mountain.
They are led by the Piper, Toffee and Egbert up the aisles of the theatre, out of the auditorium, and back to the stage.
They act crossing a very high bridge from which it is fatal to look down.
They act being scared by a monster they meet, and then act pleased when it proves to be friendly.
They act finding their way through a bottomless swamp.
They act being very cold. There is one individual line for one small child.
They join the last two lines of each verse of the Piper's song 'Secret Country' and the entire last verse.
They tell the Knight where to find the Monster.
They join in the singing of 'Inside the Mountain' and are seen in the mountain.

Scenes

ACT ONE

The River Weser
The Market Place in Hamelin
The Mayor's Dining Room

ACT TWO

SCENE ONE
The Market Place

SCENE TWO
The Shivering Bridge of Dilvergibbon
The Bottomless Swamp of Ombroglio
The Freezing Forest of Forafter
Koppelburg Mountain

Songs

ACT ONE

1.	Hamelin Town	*Toffee and Cast*
2.	If I had a big bass drum	*Piper and Band*
3.	Tramp shoving	*Boggle and Goggle*
4.	Something	*Piper and Lamplighters*
5.	Ratting it up	*King Rat and the Rodents*
6.	River water	*Toffee*
7.	Top quality	*Stallholders*
8.	The celebrated Saveloys	*Baron, Mayoress, Egbert and Townsfolk*
9.	Bring on the food	*Baron, Mayoress and Egbert*
10.	Fly away	*Toffee*
11.	Get weaving	*Nutter, Cosima and Townsfolk*
12.	Pestilential parasites	*Piper, Saveloys and Townsfolk*
13.	Gorgonzola moon	*King Rat and Massed Rats*
14.	Good riddance	*Baron and Townsfolk*

ACT TWO

15.	School song	*Mayoress, Egbert and Pupils*
16.	Ronnie the rusty robot	*Piper, Toffee and Pupils*
17.	Patchwork rap	*Piper, Toffee and Children*
18.	Gone missing	*Saveloys and Townsfolk*
19.	Secret country	*Piper and Children*
20.	Reunion opera	*Monster and Knight*
21.	Koppelburg mountain	*Toffee, Townsfolk and Audience*
22.	Inside the mountain	*Toffee*
23.	Pay the Piper	*Saveloys and Townsfolk*
24.	Inside the mountain (Reprise)	*Toffee, Piper, Egbert and Children*

Characters

The Pied Piper   *a stranger, also known as the Mystery Tramp*
Toffee Jenkins   *a young girl with a bad leg*
Cosima Beamer   *who keeps a junk and antiques stall*
Doctor Mungadory   *a learned seller of potions*
Arianalla Skiller   *who runs a toy stall*
Nutter Mausenheimer   *a miller and baker*
Boggle   *a heavy security person*
Goggle   *another of the same*
Baron Dennis Saveloy   *the Mayor of Hamelin*
Mayoress – The Lady Lucy Saveloy   *Principal of her own private school*
The Honourable Egbert Saveloy   *their only son*
Two lamplighters   *one tall and one short*
King Rat   *the Elvis of the sewer system*
The Rodents   *a Rat 'n' Roll group*
The Massed Rats   *a swarm of rats*
Pupils   *children at the Mayoress's school*
The Rampant Umbrage   *a monster*
The Iced Knight   *a female knight in armour*
The Hamelin Town Band

Act 1

[*The market place in Hamelin. Downstage right a weeping willow tree at the edge of the stage.* (TOFFEE's *boat is set under this, hidden by the leaves)*]

[CAST *enter behind market stalls which stand in a semi-circle on stage*]

[TOFFEE, *a young girl with a bad leg, enters through the middle of the market and stands centre stage*]

Toffee and Cast   [*Sing*]
Hamelin Town's in Brunswick
By famous Hanover City;
The river Weser, deep and wide,
Washes its walls on the southern side;
A pleasanter spot you never spied;
But, when begins my ditty,
Almost five hundred years ago,
To see the townsfolk suffer so
From vermin, was a pity.

Rats!
They fought the dogs, and killed the cats,
And bit the babies in the cradles,
And ate the cheeses out of the vats,
And licked the soup from the cook's own ladles,
Split open the kegs of salted sprats,
Made nests inside men's Sunday hats,
And even spoiled the women's chats,
By drowning their speaking
With shrieking and squeaking
In fifty different sharps and flats.
Rats! Rats! Rats! Rats! Rats!

[*Exit* CAST *and* TOFFEE]

[*Darkening stage. Music takes on menacing tone. Squeaks, scuffling sounds and red eyes glowing but suddenly the lights come up*]

[*Enter, playing, the* TOWN BAND – *Bass drum, trumpet, trombone, accordion and saxophone*]

[*Enter, following them like a small boy trying to keep up with a procession,* THE PIED PIPER *dressed as a Mystery Tramp, with a long overcoat and battered hat*]

Piper   [*Sings*]
                     I always wanted an instrument
                     An instrument to play
                     But my pocket money was always spent
                     On pocket money day
                     But –

                     If I had a big bass drum
                     I would wear my big bass drum-boots

Drum   Tirrum tiddle um tum tum

Piper   Like a giant in gumboots
                     I would thump it
                     You'd have to lump it
                     If you didn't like it, chum,
                     If I had a big bass
                     Twice as big as your face
                     If I had a big bass drum.

                     If I had a slide trombone
                     I would set the people howling

Trombone   Bordle ordle om pom pone

Piper   Like a lion growling
                     Kids would hear me
                     Come out and cheer me
                     And I'd make the grown-ups groan
                     If I had a trambone
                     Hotter than a hambone
                     If I had a slide trombone

                     [*The next two verses were omitted in the National Theatre production. They are included here as possible substitutes if you have no trombone or saxophone. However three instrument verses are enough*]

                     If I played accordion
                     It would be extremely pleasing

Accordion   Wa-nanna Wa-nanna Wa-won

Piper	That's my squeeze-box squeezing
	At my squozes
	You'd tap your toeses
	You'd go dancing on and on
	If I had a squeeze-box
	Louder than a sneeze-box
	If I played accordion
	If I was a trumpet man
	I would tantara and toot it
Trumpet	Tun tiddle ran tan tan
Piper	No I'd never mute it
	I would blow it
	Sweet as a poet
	Powerful as Desperate Dan
	If I had a trumpet
	I would never dump it
	If I was a trumpet man
Piper	If I had a saxophone
	I'd be very glad to puff it
Saxophone	Doodle oodle oodle own
Piper	Don't tell me to stuff it!
	Celebrations!
	Standing ovations!
	Better than a crown and throne!
	If I was a sax-man,
	Madder than an axe-man,
	If I had a saxophone
	Yes I always wanted an instrument
	An instrument to play
	But my pocket money was always spent
	On pocket money day
	And all my mother gave to me
	When I left Gomzooley Bay
	Was a pat on the head
	And a word of advice
	And a magical pipe to play . . .

[BAND *leave* PIPER *to take up the positions where they will remain for the rest of the show. They should be visible whenever relevant*]

	[*The Piper goes into a spectacular solo on the pipe, which seems to take on a life of its own. In the National Theatre production the pipe was a Lyricon, played by the saxophone player and mimed by the Piper and this double act was not concealed from the audience. Eventually the Piper, after an acrobatic solo, sits, exhausted*]
Piper	[*Noticing audience*] Good morning! Good grief! We haven't met, have we? Some folk call me – The Mystery Tramp. But they're wrong. This is just my Mystery Tramp disguise. As Mr Robert Browning says in his famous poem:

I chiefly use my piping charm
On creatures that do people harm,
The mole and toad and newt and viper;
And people call me – [*Pauses to think*]

Audience	The Pied Piper!
Piper	Shh! Yes, the Pied Piper. If people know who I really am, they bother me blue. "Please Mr Piper, please, please, please! There's bugs in our rugs and lice in our rice and fleas all over Aunt Louise!" Thing is, I'm tired to me teeth with pest control. I fancy retiring to a very comfortable mountain round here. Called the Koppelburg.

[*Enter, behind him,* BOGGLE *and* GOGGLE, *two tough security persons with helmets and uniforms. They are in charge of law and order in Hamelin. They are very used to operating as a team with a tendency to move in unison and finish each other's sentences. They move suspiciously in on the* PIPER]

Boggle	Hang a
Goggle	Bout a bit
Boggle	Who's this
Goggle	Geezer?
Boggle	I wouldn't
Goggle	Know mate
Boggle	Nor would
Goggle	I chum
Boggle	Better
Goggle	Have a word
Boggle	And get his
Goggle	Number and so on.

Boggle	[*To* PIPER] Passport
Goggle	Me old son
Boggle	We want to check
Goggle	Your whatsits!
Piper	I done nothing
Boggle	Not much you haven't
Goggle	You was blowing a pipe
Boggle	Without a licence.
Goggle	You can't make music
Boggle	If you've not got a licence. [*Takes the pipe from the* PIPER] A silvery pipe.
Goggle	That's a bit of all right.
Boggle	Probably tin.
Goggle	Chuck it into the bin. [BOGGLE *pockets the pipe*]
Piper	Who are you two?
Boggle	We're law and order
Goggle	Could get nasty
Boggle	Get the picture?
Piper	I get the picture.
Goggle	His name's Boggle
Boggle	He's called Goggle
Goggle	And we don't like strangers
Boggle	And we don't like trouble
Goggle	Passport, Sunny Jim
Boggle	At the double.
Piper	It's a very boring passport. And I didn't expect –
Boggle	It's not what you expect
Goggle	It's what you get and
Boggle	What you get in Hamelin's
Goggle	The unexpected!
Piper	I'll find it, don't worry.

Boggle	O we won't worry
Goggle	It's you that needs to worry
Boggle and Goggle	
	Just find that passport – Find it in a hurry.
Piper	Got it!

[*Hands over a shabby passport.* BOGGLE *and* GOGGLE *examine it*]

Boggle	Where was he born?
Goggle	It says: in bed.
Boggle	What's his name?
Goggle	It says: he lost it.
Boggle	What's his job?
Goggle	A mystery tramp.
Boggle	Hamelin don't want any mysteries.
Goggle	Hamelin don't want any tramp.
Boggle and Goggle	
	Tramps get thrown in the River Weser.
Piper	Don't do that!
Boggle and Goggle	
	Why not?
Piper	Rivers is damp.

[BOGGLE *and* GOGGLE *throw the* PIPER *in the river. Big splash effect*]

[BOGGLE *and* GOGGLE *sing and dance as they exit*]

Boggle	Makes me feel as sharp as a razor
Boggle and Goggle	
	Shoving of a tramp in the River Weser
Goggle	Makes me feel bright as a laser
Boggle and Goggle	
	Shoving of a tramp in the River Weser
	Shoving of a
	Shoving of a
	Shoving of a
	Shoving of a
	Shoving of a tramp in the River Weser!

[PIPER *emerges from the river. It's getting dark*]

Piper   You'll be sorry! If they hadn't snaffled my pipe, I'd turn those
two into a couple of My Little Ponies. Well, Hamelin's a funny
old town. They've never met me before, but they treat me
like a total stranger.

[TWO LAMPLIGHTERS *one tall with a long pole for lighting lamps, the
other short with a short pole, enter and begin to light lamps*]

[*A rubbish cart full of dark bags is pushed on*]

[*Sings*]
Well the sun is almost setting
And the atmosphere is getting
Just a little sharp and chilly
And I know it may sound silly
But I've got a nasty feeling
There are little bodies stealing
From the mountains and the valleys
To the shadows of our alleys
And while Hamelin is sleeping
There's a crawling and a creeping
And I'm sure I heard a squeaking
Or the sound of floorboards creaking
Such a skittering and spluttering
In gardens and in guttering
And scratching and a-scritching
In the larder and the kitching
And it's –

Piper and Two Lamplighters

[*Sing*]
Something
Something
Something

Something!
Where?
Something there!
Down there!
Where?
There!

Something
Hairy
And grey
Never seen
By
Day!

Something
Brown
And long!
Something sly
And
Strong!

[LAMPLIGHTERS *see something and flee, leaving* PIPER *alone without knowing he's alone*]

Piper   [*Sings*]
In sewers
In fountains
In hundreds
In thousands
They whisper
They fizzle
They hiss and
They drizzle
They bristle
They amble
They slither
They scramble

Something
Something
Something . . .

[*Speaks*]
Walloping werewolves – I'm well terrified. But where in
    Hamelin can I hide?

[*Looks in rubbish cart*]

Ah! Looks like a mound of hairclippings left on the
    barbershop floor after twenty barbers have been clipping
    and cropping all day. A great big heap of hair.

[*Climbs onto the heap in the cart*]

Piper   Just like a sofa! Funny. It's moving! It's alive!

[*Exit, fast, the* PIPER]

[*The pile becomes a group of super-rats, fast moving with clacking
jaws and shining eyes and swishing tails which they use like
microphones. They are led by* KING RAT *who is a kind of Elvis
Presley/Little Richard figure. The whole group is known as* KING RAT
AND THE RODENTS]

King	[*Speaks*]

King

[*Speaks*]
C'mon everybody
Slap some grease on those paws
Get some yellow on your teeth
And, uh, sharpen up your claws

There's a whole lot of sausage
We're gonna swallow down
[*Sings*]
We're gonna jump out the sewers
And rock this town.

King and Rodents

Cos we're ratting it up
Yes we're ratting it up
Well we're ratting it up
For a ratting good time tonight.

[RATS *begin to break up the town. During the number there are more and more sounds of glass and crockery smashing, squeaks, barking, babies crying etc – mainly in between the verses*]

King

Ain't got no compass
You don't need no map
Just follow your snout
Hey, watch out for that trap!

You can take out a poodle
Beat up a cat
But if you can't lick a ferret
You ain't no kind of rat.

King and Rodents

Cos we're ratting it up
Yes we're ratting it up
Well we're ratting it up
For a ratting good time tonight.

[*Sax solo*]

King

Now you can sneak in the henhouse
You can roll out the eggs
But if the farmer comes running
Bite his hairy legs

Check that cheese for poison
Before you eat
Or you'll wind up being served up
As ratburger meat.

King and Rodents

> Cos we're ratting it up
> Yes we're ratting it up
> Well we're ratting it up
> For a ratting good time tonight.

King

> This rat was born to rock
> This rat was born to roll
> I don't give a monkey's
> Bout your pest control
>
> So push off pussy-cat
> And push off pup
> We're the Rocking Rodents
> And we're ratting it up.

King and Rodents

> Yeah we're ratting it up
> Yeah we're ratting it up
> Well we're ratting it up
> For a ratting good time tonight!

[Big climax]

[One RODENT *finds the pipe in a dustbin and presents it to* KING RAT. *He sniffs it but throws it away in disgust. It is caught craftily by the* PIPER, *who appears just in time, then vanishes, gleefully, with the pipe]*

*[*KING RAT *and the* RODENTS *bow and exit underground. The sound of ratty laughter is heard]*

[Lights up on the weeping willow which is downstage right]

[Emerging from under it comes a small green boat. TOFFEE JENKINS, *a young girl with a bad leg, sails it slowly to the centre of the stage, singing as she travels]*

Toffee

> *[Sings]*
> River water
> Carry me along
> In the shadow
> Of the river trees
> River water
> Cool and green and strong
> Waterbirds are playing
> On your river breeze

Where I come from
I don't remember
Where I'm going
I do not care
River water
Carry me along
To a happy landing
To a job and lodgings
Somewhere

River water
Carry me along
Watching fishes
Skim the river bed
River water
Sing your river song
Of the creatures swimming
In your glassy head

Oh where I come from
I don't remember
Where I'm going
I do not care
River water
Carry me along
To a happy landing
And some work to do
And a bed to sleep in
And a good hot breakfast
Somewhere

[TOFFEE *ties up her boat and steps ashore. Immediately the market stalls spring to life. Stallholders with spectacular barrows are crying their wares.* COSIMA BEAMER *is a sour woman who runs a junk and antiques stall.* DOCTOR MUNGADORY *is a learned old man who sells patent medicines of all kinds.* ARIANALLA SKILLER *is the warm-hearted toy stall keeper.* NUTTER MAUSENHEIMER *is a miller who runs a bakery stall. After crying their wares from their stalls they converge on* TOFFEE, *becoming more and more insistent that she buy something. She feels like Alice in Wonderland, menaced by these strangers*]

Cosima	Antiques and bric a brac!
Doctor	Mungadory's Marvellous Medicine!

Arianalla	Toys for everyone!
Nutter	Doughnuts! Doughnuts!
Stallholders	All top quality No trash We got the goods If you got the cash
Cosima	Here's the original Mona Lisa And a BMX ridden by Julius Caesar
Doctor	Mungadory's Medicine Makes the sickly well If you pinch your nostrils It's hardly got a smell
Arianalla	Dolls that walk Dolls that talk Dolls that eat With a knife and fork
Nutter	Buy a loaf of bread Bigger than your head Nowt taken out But an old Brussels sprout
Stallholders	All top quality No trash We got the goods If you got the cash
Cosima	Teddy bears with one eye Teddy bears with two If you don't buy a teddy bear A bear will swallow you
Doctor	Professor Popple's Pepper Pills for People who turn Purple!
Arianalla	Water-pistols Fill 'em from a glass Squirt your teacher From right across the class
Nutter	Swiss Roll! Swiss Roll! From last week's market. You could unroll it And use it for a carpet

[*Enter* BOGGLE *and* GOGGLE *twirling long truncheons*]

Stallholders All top quality
No trash
We got the goods
If you got the cash . . .

Toffee [*Breaking out of the crowd*] Stop! I don't want anything.

All You must want something.

Toffee Well I do. But I've got no money.

All She's got no money.

Doctor No money won't get you far in Hamelin.

Boggle What's your name?

Toffee I'm Toffee Jenkins.

Goggle Where are you from?

Toffee I can't remember.

Boggle You can't remember?

Goggle What can you remember?

Toffee I was in a green boat. Yes a boat on the river.

Boggle On the <u>river</u>?

Goggle You travelled on the <u>river</u>?

Toffee What's wrong with that?

Boggle and Goggle

All the water in the river
From here to there
All the water in the river
Belongs to the Mayor

Arianalla And here he comes
Like a grizzly bear!

[*The* BARON, *the* MAYORESS *and their spoilt son* EGBERT *walk down the aisle towards the stage.* EGBERT *wears a sailor suit and shoots the audience with a water gun. All burst into song*]

All [*Except* TOFFEE]
Let the Hamelin band
Make one heck of a noise
And deafen everyone
For here come the celebrated Saveloys

Egbert   And here comes their only son!

Baron   I am the Mayor
And you'd better take care
If there's anything you've done
Or left undone
For the Mayor will pounce on you

Mayoress   And I will bounce on you

Egbert   And so will their only son!

Mayoress   I'm the Mayoress
And I couldn't care less
If I tread upon your toes
And spoil your fun

Baron and Mayoress
You can hate the two of us
But when you are through with us

Egbert   You'll still have their only son!

Baron and Mayoress
Let the Hamelin Band
Make one heck of a noise
Blow up the big trombun
For here come the celebrated Saveloys

Egbert   And here comes their only son!
I'm their pride and joy
I'm Egbert Saveloy
And I'll shoot you in the face
With my custard gun

Baron   So the Mayor will jeer at you

Mayoress   His wife will sneer at you

Egbert   And so will their only son!

All   Let the Hamelin Band
Make one heck of a noise
And deafen everyone
For here come the celebrated Saveloys!

Egbert   And here comes their only son!

[MAYORESS *approaches* COSIMA*'s junk stall*]

Mayoress   My goodness me, Cosima Beamer, what a delightful selection
of antiques, bric-a-brac, oddments and junk.

Cosima	All good stuff, Lady Saveloy. Highest quality, lowest prices.
Mayoress	Oh prices, it doesn't do to worry about prices. No, when I take a fancy to something I simply have to have it and to Hammersmith with the price.
Cosima	Yes of course, Lady Saveloy. If I find anything that suits you I'll certainly put it aside for you.
Mayoress	You don't mind if I hover, do you?
	[COSIMA *is trying to put away the most valuable things*]
Cosima	Oh no, hover away.
Mayoress	[*Pouncing*] Ah! Oh! Exquisite!
Cosima	I'm afraid that's a bit pricey.
Mayoress	What a beautiful necklace!
Cosima	Seventy-five is the least I could possibly –
Mayoress	What a beautiful necklace!
Cosima	I mean, it cost me seventy and I have to pay the rent for my stall and –
Mayoress	Look, Dennis, look – a beautiful necklace.
Baron	Beautiful necklace, dearest.
	[COSIMA *reluctantly puts the necklace round the* MAYORESS*'s neck*]
Mayoress	How does it look on me, Mrs Beamer?
Cosima	Like a river of blue fire.
	[MAYORESS *simpers and turns away*]
Cosima	[*Aside*] Round the neck of a giant slug.
	[BARON *is engaging in somewhat furtive conversation with* DOCTOR MUNGADORY]
Baron	Did you manage to find me a potion?
Doctor	Now where did I put it? Ah, here we are. Doctor Mungadory's Good Temper Powder. Just sprinkle this on the wrong side of the bed while she's asleep and all the next day she'll be as sweet as marzipan.
Baron	That's not the one I mean, Mungadory. I mean the potion that will rid Hamelin of the Fear.
Doctor	The Fear, Baron?

Baron	Yes the ferocious Fear that creeps into Hamelin every night.
	[DOCTOR *looks puzzled*]
Doctor	The ferocious Fear with forty thousand feet?
Baron	Shhh. Everybody gets angry when rats are mentioned round here. Now, Mungadory, where's the medicine to cure that <u>Fear</u>?
Doctor	My apologies, Baron, I can't find anything for it.
Baron	Bramblehead! Puddingbrain!
Doctor	Sir, I am a scientist and a respected inventor.
Baron	Well invent something! Quick!
	[EGBERT *and* MAYORESS *have approached* ARIANALLA*'s toy stall*]
Egbert	Mum, mum, look at that robot! It changes itself into a space rocket and the space rocket turns itself into a bazooka-firing tank and the bazooka-firing tank turns itself into a nuclear submarine.
Mayoress	Oh, and what does the nuclear submarine turn itself into?
Arianalla	A lovely cuddly bunny rabbit.
Egbert	Oh mum, mum, it's a brilliant robot.
Mayoress	He'll have to wait until his birthday, won't he Arianalla?
Egbert	Oh mum! [*Begins to howl*]
Baron	What's up with our Egbert, mother?
Arianalla	Here, Egbert, have your birthday now. [*Gives him the robot. Aside*] I hope it turns itself into a vampire and sucks you white.
Mayoress	Many thanks, Arianalla, say thank you Egbert.
Egbert	Thank you Egbert! I'll be back next week, Mrs Skiller.
	[EGBERT *and* MAYORESS *join* BARON *at* NUTTER*'s bakery stall*]
Baron	Now don't let's have hard words, Mr Mausenheimer.
Nutter	Hard words in hard times, that's what I say, Mr Mayor. Now as you know I pride myself on three things: I'm a hard-working miller, a top-class baker and a blunt man. And I say you've got to do something about the rats!
Cosima	Yes – get those rats dealt with – NOW!
Citizens	Rats out! Save our city! Rats out! Save our city!

Boggle	Now watch it.
Goggle	Citizens.
Boggle	Calm down
Goggle	The lot of you.
Mayoress	Better make one of your speeches, dear.
Baron	Citizens of Hamelin – all these rumours of rats in the night are a right load of old haddockswallop. Hamelin is a stuperiferous town and I am a Mayor in a million. All our people are happy, beautifully-housed, marvellously fed and fully employed. Just like the people of England.
Toffee	Excuse me, sir, but I heard what you said. I've been travelling ever since I can remember and I'm tired and hungry. Hamelin seems such a friendly, magical town. I'd like to stay. Please can you help me find some work to do, a bed to sleep in and a good hot breakfast?
Baron	Now just a moment, young woman. You can't just barge into town and demand a job.
Nutter	What about that full employment?
Egbert	She's all grubby. And raggedy.
Mayoress	Give her a job.
Baron	What for?
Mayoress	It'll look good in the Hamelin Herald. Besides, I need a cook and a waitress and a sweeper-upper and a bedmaker and a general Cinderella.
Baron	You're hired.
Toffee	Oh thank you, sir.
Egbert	What's your name?
Toffee	Toffee Jenkins.
Egbert	I'm the Honourable Egbert Saveloy.
Mayoress	Let's go home, Dennis. There's golden soup and stargazy pie and boa constrictor steaks and stripey trifle for tea.
Toffee	That sounds great.
Mayoress	It'd better be. You're cooking it.

[*Exit* BARON, MAYORESS, EGBERT *and* TOFFEE]

Nutter	Enjoy your meal – if the rats don't get it first!
Cosima	Rats out! Save our city!
	[BOGGLE *and* GOGGLE *converge on* COSIMA]
Boggle	We said cool down
Goggle	And we meant cool down
Boggle	You'd better watch it.
Goggle	If you know what's bad for you.
Nutter	Boggle and Goggle, why don't you do something?
Cosima	You're meant to be in charge of law and order.
Boggle	Don't start on us.
Goggle	We're not rat catchers.
Boggle	All we can do
Goggle	Is make a report
Boggle	That's right, we make a report to the Mayor
Goggle	And the Mayor will do what the Mayor will do.
	[*Exit* BOGGLE *and* GOGGLE]
	[DOCTOR MUNGADORY *produces a copy of Hamelin Herald*]
Doctor	[*Reading headline*] RATS ON THE RAMPAGE! BOOMTOWN RATS!
Cosima	Tell us, Doctor, what's the answer to that?
Nutter	We've heard of giant rats, but these were the giantest. What's your opinion as an eminent scientist?
Doctor	The rat, or more correctly, Rattus Rattus, can have as many as fifty babies a year. When these are six months old, they can have babies of their own. Within ten years, if nothing prevents them, the entire world will be covered with rats.
Cosima	We don't want a lecture. We want action.
Doctor	But what can we do? Traps don't work. Our rats are too clever – they warn each other.
Nutter	Poison?
Doctor	With poison they die under the floorboards and make a horrible smell.

Cosima	We've got to do something.
Nutter and Cosima	
	We've got to get rid of the rats!
Doctor	Well Hamelin is historically a very democratic town. So let's vote on how to get rid of the rats.
Cosima	Good idea!
Arianalla	I think all these people ought to have a vote. [*Indicating audience*]
Cosima	Oh they don't want a vote. Do you?
	[*Audience response*]
Nutter	All right, who's got an idea?
Cosima	Why don't we get some really fierce weasels to chase out the rats?
Doctor	How would we get rid of the weasels?
Cosima	With ferocious dogs.
Nutter	What would we do with the dogs?
Cosima	Vicious snakes.
Arianalla	I don't want to be awkward, but how'd we get rid of the snakes?
Cosima	Crocodiles, stupid.
Doctor	Hmmmmmm. I have been considering considerably and I have come to an astoundishing conclusion.
All	What's that, Doctor Mungadory?
Doctor	I think we should all go to the town football pitch with shovels and dig a gynormous hole and hide at the bottom of it till the rats get fed up and go away. I'm not a scaredy cat, just sensible.
Arianalla	Let's just go and see the Mayor and tell him to get rid of the rats. He's meant to look after us.
Nutter	Let's take a vote. If you agree with an idea, put your right hand in the air. And if you agree with an idea very much, put both hands in the air. Remember you can only vote for one of the three ideas. Cosima!
Cosima	Who votes for weasels to chase out the rats?
	[*Count*]

Nutter   180! Doctor Mungadory?

Doctor   Who votes for hiding in a gynormous hole?

                  [*Count*]

Nutter   77!

Arianalla   Who votes for going to see that old Mayor and telling him to
                  get rid of the rats. Or we'll get rid of him and his greedy wife
                  and soppy son. Who votes for that?

                  [*Count*]

Nutter   Eight hundred and eighty eight! All right, we'll go and see the
                  Mayor. We'll just run home to collect some banners. Then
                  we'll march on the Town Hall and tell the Mayor what's what.

All   What's what!

                  [*Exit all*]

                  [*Lighting down on the market square*]

                  [*Lighting up on area which represents the banqueting room of the
                  Town Hall.* BARON, MAYORESS *and* EGBERT *sit at table*]

Egbert   Mum! I'm hungry, Mum!

Mayoress   I'm hungry too, my darling. I could eat a dinosaur.

Baron   Where's me turtle soup? I don't feel like a Mayor without me
                  turtle soup!

Mayoress   It's that new girl, Toffee. She's so slow.

Baron   Where is that girl?

Egbert   Mum! I think I'm going to die of starvation!

                  [*The* SAVELOYS *sing*]

Baron   Steaks by the score

Egbert   Burgers galore

Mayoress   I love the smell of meat, sir!

Baron   Buckets of chips!

Egbert   Good for the hips!

Mayoress   Bring me a tower of pizza!

                  [TOFFEE *begins to bustle on and off carrying plates piled high with
                  rich and luxurious food. The* SAVELOYS *tuck in*]

Saveloys	Bring on the food I'm in the mood Bring on the jugs of vino Nip down the pub Get some more grub We'll have a right old beano!
Baron	Prawn vindaloo? Yes, that'll do.
Egbert	My stomach's trying to break out!
Baron	Fetch a jugged hare
Mayoress	And, while you're there Bring me a Chinese take out!
Saveloys	Bring on the food I'm in the mood Bring on the jugs of vino Nip down the pub Get some more grub We'll have a right old beano!
Toffee	[*Sings*] Fat as lard And rich as gravy This family Drives me crazy
	Faster girl And then they blame me For breakages – Drives me barmy –
	But one day soon I'm going to spread my wings and fly away Anywhere anywhere far away One day soon I'm going to spread my wings and fly away Fly away
	Slick and thick And sly and sloppy This family Drives me potty
	Rude as rats And mean as bankers They're trying to Drive me bonkers

But one day soon I'm going to spread my wings and fly away
Anywhere anywhere far away
One day soon I'm going to spread my wings and fly away
Fly away, fly away . . .

Mayoress   I have a dream
Cream cakes with cream

Egbert   Mind, or you'll get an eyeful!

Baron   Pass the eclairs!
Slice me some pears!

Mayoress   Bring me a trayful of trifle!

Saveloys   Bring on the food
I'm in the mood
Bring on the jugs of vino
Nip down the pub
Get some more grub
We'll have a right old beano!

Baron   You'll have to do better than this, you know.

Mayoress   Or you'll be getting the old heave-ho.

Egbert   I'll be sorry if you have to go.

Toffee   I'll do my best, that's all I can do.

Mayoress   You'll do better than that – or it's out with you.

Baron   Next time stick more wine in the venison stew.

Egbert   Do you like monster? I've got a craze on monsters and my
hobby is monster-spotting and I get the Creature Magazine
every week and I always carry a copy of the Monster Book
of Monsters by Emma Shuddering and one Saturday you can
come with me down to Slaughteroo Station to watch the
zombies arrive.

Mayoress   That's enough.

Baron   She's just a servant.

Mayoress   Don't distract her from her duties.

Toffee   I'm very sorry to interrupt feeding time, but there are about a
thousand angry citizens outside your window and they want
to tell you something or other.

[*Lights up on Market Square*]

[*Citizens, led by* NUTTER *and* COSIMA *carry protest banners and march to music until they stand below the room where the* SAVELOYS *are eating*]

[*Banners include RATS OUT! SAVE OUR CITY, and held by the* DOCTOR, *RID US OF THESE RODENTS, PLEASE*]

[COSIMA, NUTTER *and* TOWNSFOLK *sing*]

Nutter

We've been paying plenty
For rates and fares and such
Taxes got worse
As you lined your purse
But none of us grumbled much

Cosima

Now we're paying double
Because of pesky rats
Bashing our kids
And our dustbin lids
And beating up our dogs and cats

Cosima, Nutter, Townsfolk

Get weaving
Or start leaving
You know what we mean
Get cracking
Or start packing
We want a town that's clean.

While they claw us
You ignore us
So we bellow in chorus
Like a brontosaurus:

Get weaving
Or start leaving
You know what we mean
We want a town that's clean
And a caring daring Mayor
Not a broken-down machine.

Nutter

Call this law and order?
Well I would call it war!
Start making your move
If you want to prove
What Mayors draw wages for.

Cosima	Here's our final warning And here's what you must do Get rid of the pests Get rid of their nests Or Hamelin gets rid of you.
Cosima, Nutter, Townsfolk	Get weaving Or start leaving etc . . .

[Unseen by the TOWNSFOLK *and the* SAVELOYS, *who freeze, the* PIED PIPER *appears, walking along a parapet. He wears a magical patchwork coat, a strange hat, and a shining pipe which hangs around his neck. He is smiling as he walks out of sight]*

Baron	What do I do now?
Mayoress	Play for time.
Egbert	Where's the mustard?
Baron	Ladies and gents, I understand your concern. I simply ask for ten months in which to find an answer to this problem.
Cosima	Ten months? Rats!
Nutter	We won't give you ten days.
Cosima	We'll give you ten minutes.
Nutter	Right. Ten minutes and that's your lot.
Citizens	Ten minutes and then you're out.

*[*CITIZENS *turn away and speak silently in twos and threes]*

Baron	*[Highly agitated]* What'll I do? They'll bottle me, throttle me and dump me in the river.
Mayoress	Toffee! You'd better start packing my wardrobe –
Egbert	Why have we got to leave Hamelin?
Mayoress	Because your father just can't cope.
Egbert	Can we move to Transylvania? They have lovely werewolves. And vampires too.
Baron	Shut up! I'm trying to think.

[There is a loud triple knock at the door of the SAVELOY's *home.*

Toffee	Baron Saveloy, there's somebody at the door.
Baron	Send 'em away. I've got to think fast.

[TOFFEE *goes back to the door*]

Now, perhaps I could use flame-throwers on the rats.

Mayoress   Oh yes, and burn down the town while you're about it.

Egbert   I could do with another meringue.

[*Another triple knock at the door*]

Toffee   He won't go away. He says you need him.

Baron   I don't need anyone. I just need time to think.

Mayoress   Time to think? It's time to pack. Come on!

Egbert   Cream, please.

[*Another triple knock*]

Baron   Who is it, Toffee?

Toffee   He's the strangest man I ever saw in my life . . .

Egbert   Maybe he's a monster. Let him in!

Baron   He can't make things any worse. Let him in!

Toffee   You can come in now.

[*Music*]

[*Enter the* PIPER *out of a large cake on the table. He stands on the table looking around*]

Baron   Who the Hamelin do you think you are?

Piper   My name is a secret between me and the mountain. But most people call me the Pied Piper.

Baron   Piper? What's that? You mend pipes? You're a plumber?

Egbert   The Pied Plumber?

Mayoress   You're as daft as doughnuts. He plays a pipe. [*With disgust*] He's a musician.

Egbert   No, he's a magician, aren't you mister?

Baron   Musicians, magicians, scallywags and riff-raff.

Piper   Mugical? Mazzical? Much the same animal!

Toffee   Are Magic and Music the same as each other?

Piper   Music and Magic are sister and brother, Toffee Jenkins.

Toffee   How did you know my name, Piper?

Piper   It's just one of my music tricks.

Baron   Ignore her.

Mayoress   Pretend she's invisible.

Egbert   But she's quite pretty.

Mayoress   Pretty is as pretty does, and she does pretty little. Eat up, Egbert.

Baron   Magic or music, can you help me?

Piper   Maybe. You're having rat trouble?

Baron   Terrible trouble. And if I don't find an answer within nine minutes – I'll be dumboogled.

Piper   Well – I happen to be the greatest kicker-out of pests and parasites this world has ever seen.

Mayoress   Where, when and what have you ever done?

Piper   [*Sings*]
                  Ice cream cornets
                  Nicked by hornets
                  On the Hoodoo Highways
                  But my playing
                  Set them swaying
                  Blew them out the skyways.

                  Scarlet Dragons
                  Wild as wagons
                  In the streets of Nogo.
                  Got them scooting
                  With my tooting
                  Had to dance the Go-Go.

                  [*Chorus*]
                  Pick a pestilential parasite
                  And put a little pepper on it
                  Bop it on the boko
                  Biff it boldly on the bonnet
                  And blow me if you bother him
                  He probably feels riper
                  For pestilential parasites
                  You'd better call the Piper.

Lurking leopards
Ate some shepherds
On the Hills of Hompoff.
Tootled breezily
Oh so easily
Had them dance the Stomp Off.

Green gorillas
Hairy killers
Vulture, toad and viper
Disappear
When they hear
Music by the Piper.

Piper, Saveloys and Toffee (Chorus)
Pick a pestilential parasite (etc)

Piper
Deadly hookworm
Wiggly bookworm
Bug or boa-constrictor,
Creepy-crawly –
All end poorly –
Music is the victor.

Octopuses
Big as buses
In the Lake of Loogie –
Played them bits
From all my hits and
Made them dance the boogie.

Piper and Company (Chorus)
Pick a Pestilential parasite (etc)

Baron   That's all very find and dandy. But do you know anything
about rats?

Piper   [*Laughs*] Know anything about rats? I was more or less
brought up with them. Kept a dozen pet rats when I was a lad.

Egbert   Really?

Piper   Took 'em to school to keep teacher amused.

Egbert   Didn't they bite you?

Piper   Bite me? Bless you, of course they did. It's in the nature of
your rat to bite.

Toffee   Were they bad bites?

Piper	Some were bad and none of them good. The barn rat's not so grisly, he's a plump little fellow, living off top of the wheat and dairymilk. He gives you a nice clean little nip. But your sewer rat, he's a different kettle of germs, he is. Nasty class of bite, three-cornered bite, bleeds for ever such a long time.
Mayoress	You've been bitten many times?
Piper	I've been bitten thousands, on account of me being so tasty. You see this thumbnail, bitten right through ten years ago and still got a split in it. That was the worst bite I ever got bit. The pain went shooting all the way up to my ear. Me thumb went black and I was told I ought to have it taken off, but I kept it cos I was fond of it. Had it all me life, you know. [*Sucks thumb*]
Baron	But the point is this – can you rid Hamelin of rats?
Piper	The point is – yes – easy as pie.
Mayoress	How long will it take you?
Piper	One moonlit night.
Baron	There's a moon tonight.
Piper	You'll have no rats tomorrow.
Baron	Er . . . how much do you charge?
Piper	Fifty quid cash, is that fair?
Baron	Fifty – listen, if you can get the rats out of Hamelin, I'll pay you one thousand golden pounds –
Piper	In a silken purse? Right, if that's the going rate I won't say no, on account of me being poor.
Baron	And me being rich. [*Laughs*]
Mayoress	Filthy rich.
Baron	One thousand golden pounds – it's a deal then?
Piper	It's a deal.
	[*They shake hands.* BARON *has one hand with fingers crossed behind his back*]
Baron	We'll go up to our beds, Piper, you can get down to work.
	[CITIZENS *scatter to their homes leaving* PIPER *on stage alone as he whirls round and round in a dervish dance and the lights change to night and midnight and the moon comes out. Finally, the* PIPER *comes to a standstill. The town clock strikes*]

[TOFFEE *looks out of her window. She is the only one to see the* PIPER *working*]

Toffee

[*Speaks*]
Into the street the Piper stept,
    Smiling at first a little smile,
As if he knew what magic slept
    In his quiet pipe the while.

Then, like a musical adept,
To blow the pipe his lips he wrinkled,
And green and blue his sharp eyes twinkled,
Like a candle-flame where salt is sprinkled;
And ere three shrill notes the pipe uttered,
You heard as if an army muttered:

And the muttering grew to a grumbling;
And the grumbling grew to a mighty rumbling;
And out of the houses the rats came tumbling.

[*The* PIPER *begins to play and gradually* KING RAT *and a crowd of* MASSED RATS *begin to emerge. They are enchanted by the music of the pipe and follow the* PIPER *on a winding course towards the riverside*]

Toffee

[*Speaks*]
Great rats, small rats, lean rats, brawny rats,
Brown rats, black rats, grey rats, tawny rats,
Grave old plodders, gay young friskers,
Fathers, mothers, uncles, cousins,
Cocking tails and pricking whiskers,
Families by tens and dozens,
Brothers, sisters, husbands, wives –
Followed the Piper for their lives.
From street to street he piped advancing
And step for step they followed dancing
Until they came to the riverside
Until they came to the riverside
And the moon shone down on their revelries
And the rats all knew that the moon was made of cheese . . .

[*The* MASSED RATS *succumb to the illusion that the river, which runs past the town, and which we see shining, is made of molten cheese. The* PIPER *leads them to the riverbank and they drown very happily in the waters*]

King Rat and Massed Rats

[*Sing*]
Gorgonzola Moon
I am shaking like jelly
As your moonbeams turn
The river to cheese.

Gorgonzola Moon
You're as bright as the telly
You're as nice as lice
And you're as friendly as fleas.

I take one sniff of you
And I'm ready to take a chance
Just one sweet sniff of you
And I'm singing a song
Another sniff of you
And I'm ready to break-a dance
When I sniff a whiff
Of your wonderful pong.

Gorgonzola Moon
Shine down on my belly
Let your perfume fly
On the riverside breeze

Gorgonzola Moon
You're so beautifully smelly
That I'm glad to drown
Down in the river of cheese

Yes I'm happy to drown
Going down going down
Happy to drown
Down in the river
In the river of melted cheese –

Last Surviving Rat

Gorgonzola Moon . . .
[*Expires*]

[*Finally the* PIPER *walks away over the river and up the aisle,
playing his pipe*]

[*Suddenly it is morning. The* SAVELOYS *and all* CITIZENS *run down
to the riverbank, stare down at the drowned rats and cheer. They
crowd round to congratulate the* BARON, *who leads them in a song*]

Baron and Citizens

> They gave us
> Some bad moments
> Good riddance
> To bad rodents
> They acted
> Beelzebubbish
> Good riddance
> To bad rubbish
>
> Now they've gone
> With the gruesome garbage
> Knotted tails and
> Whiskers curled
> Now we'll throw
> The mightiest party
> Ever seen
> In the beano-loving world.

Egbert   Give us a countdown on what we'll need for
the celebrations, Mr Mayor Dad!

[BARON *barks out the numbers,* CITIZENS *respond with the rest of each line...*]

Baron and Citizens

> Ten   thousand balloons
> Nine   crazy buffoons
> Eight   miles of festoons
> Seven   lazy lagoons
> Six   thousand soup spoons
> Five   shiny spittoons
> Four   hundred doubloons
> Three   B-flat bassoons
> Two   pink macaroons
> And one
> One
> Smiling sun
> And a million marvellous moons
>
> They gave us
> Some bad moments
> Good riddance
> To bad rodents
> They acted

Beelzebubbish
Good riddance
To bad rubbish
[*Repeat*]

But now they've gone!
Gone! Gone!

Mayoress   We're going to celebrate.

Egbert   See you all in fifteen minutes.

Baron and Mayoress
        EGBERT!

[*Exeunt – exultant*]

End of Act One

Act 2

Scene One

[*The Market Square. Bright and cheerful. Bunting, balloons and banners*]

[MAYORESS, *now wearing academic gown and hat plus a rat stole, and* EGBERT, *wearing the school uniform, lead on a gloomy crocodile of* PUPILS. *Each of them wears the school uniform, a long, dark and all-enveloping cloak*]

Pupils   [*Arriving in crocodile from distance*]
The Lady Lucy Saveloy's
Remarkable Academy
For Children of Respectable Folk.
Every child is full of joy
Yes every child is glad to be
A wearer of the Saveloy Cloak.

Now every day we're good as gold
And every day do what we're told,
You couldn't meet with happier folk
At Lady Lucy Saveloy's
Remarkable Academy
For Children of Respectable Folk.

Mayoress   Sing up children!

Mayoress and Pupils
How we love our teacher!
How we love our school!
How we love our lovely teacher!
How we love our lovely school!

Mayoress   Dear children
Their cheeks are like roses.
(Darren, I'll behead you
If you do that to Jane.)
Dear children
Such sweet little noses!
(Sally, you'll be strangled
If you fidget again.)

I love them
They're sweeter than honey
(Stop it, Mary, or I'll
Nail you up in the Park.)
Their parents
Are dripping with money!
How I love those parents –
(Take your finger out Mark!)

Mayoress and Pupils

Now every day we're good as gold
And every day do what we're told,
You couldn't meet with happier folk,
At Lady Lucy Saveloy's
Remarkable Academy
For Children of Respectable Folk.

Mayoress and Pupils

[*As* EGBERT *holds up a blackboard*]
How we love our teacher
How we love our school!
How we love our lovely teacher!
How we love our lovely school!

[EGBERT *reverses the blackboard and the* PUPILS *sing*]

Pupils   How we love our peanuts!
How we love our chips!
How we love our lovely pizza!
How we love our bubblegum!

Mayoress   Enough! Children! Asseyez vous!

Children   What?

Mayoress   Sit! And now we come to the announcement that you've all been waiting for – the winner of the Lady Saveloy Prize for Beautiful Poetry. Toffee!

[*Huge cup is brought on by* TOFFEE]

Bring it over here, girl. Don't drop the lid, it's solid silver.
Doctor Mungadory, the envelope, if you please.

Doctor   What an excitement! You could hear an elephant drop.

Mayoress   And the winner of the Lady Saveloy Cup for Beautiful Poetry is – [*Opens envelope and gasps*] – the Honourable Egbert Saveloy.

[*Sparse applause*]

	[*Shaking hands with* EGBERT] Egbert, would you like to read us your beautiful poem?
Egbert	No, Mum, I've written an even more beautiful one.
Mayoress	My clever little Eggy!
	[EGBERT *takes out a scroll and coughs and reads*]
Egbert	This is a very beautiful poem by the Honourable Egbert Saveloy and it is called – School Dinners. Lumpy custard and liver – ugh! I hate school dinners and I'll tell you why – There's dog food with peas in, There's Secret Stew, And a cheese and bacon thing we call Sick Pie.
Mayoress	Egbert, that is utterly revolting! You forfeit the Cup!
Egbert	Oh, Mum!
Mayoress	But now let us give a tumultuous welcome to the man who has rid us of the rats. Pray be upstanding for the Hero of Hamelin.
	[ALL, *expecting the* PIPER, *cheer loudly. Cheering changes to boos and grumbles as the* BARON *is brought in by* BOGGLE *and* GOGGLE, *riding on the decorated rubbish cart, which is now carrying a banner saying LONG LIVE OUR GRACIOUS MARE!*]
Baron	Thank you very much my humble subjects and objects. You may be seated if you have the wherewithal on which to do so. This is indeed a day of rejoicement and merrybubble. You do right to celebrate, Hamelin people! Ring those bells till they rock that steeple!
	[DOCTOR MUNGADORY *rushes up to the* BARON *excitedly with a copy of the Hamelin Herald*]
Doctor	BARON KICKS OUT RATS! How did you manage it, your honour?
Baron	You know me, Mungadory, I'm not a chap for blowing my own trumpet, but I do feel that this was a triumph for strong leadership –
Mayoress	– And teamwork. My husband and I spent many sleepless nights drawing up a plan of action –
Baron	– And then it was a question of waiting, despite the impatience of some of our citizens [*This at* NUTTER *and* COSIMA] for the right moment to strike, and when that moment came –

Mayoress   – I gave the word – and the entire monstrous army of rats –

Egbert   – Got drownded in the river by the Pied Piper.

Mayoress   Fold up, Egbert!

Doctor   So? It was the work of this mysterious stranger?

Baron   Well I was aided to some extent by the so-called Pied Spider –

Mayoress   Spiced Paper –

Piper   [*Stepping in between them from nowhere*] Pied Piper.

Egbert   Mr Piper, will you stay for lunch with us?

Piper   Well, I'm in a bit of a rush because I've had a call in from Timbuctoo about a plague of scorpions, so I'd better be on my way –

Baron   Well thanks very much, and toodle-oo!

Mayoress   So nice knowing you.

Piper   I don't like to bring it up, but just before I toodle-oo, what about me wages?

Baron   Of course. Fifty quid cash, I think you said?

Piper   One thousand golden pounds. We shook on that.

Toffee   One thousand golden pounds in a silken purse.

Baron   Keep out of this, girl.

Mayoress   One thousand pounds – the Mayor was joking –

Baron   Of course I was joking –

Mayoress   Can't you take a joke?

Baron   Come on, take fifty and on your bike.

Piper   We shook on a thousand.

Nutter   Lord Saveloy, don't you think we ought to pay up? For the honour of Hamelin?

Cosima   A promise is a promise. You'll have to pay up.

Citizens   That's right. Pay up. Pay the Piper etc . . .

Baron   Now, just a moment. Hold your hedgehogs. It's not me that's paying. It's not my money. It's Hamelin's money. Your money. If we pay the piper a thousand golden pounds, you know what it means? You'll pay twice the taxes and triple the rates.

Nutter	We'll have to pay?
Cosima	That's impossible.
Arianalla	We can't afford a thousand.
Cosima	Nowise, nohow.
Mayoress	One thousand pounds? Don't make me laugh!
Baron	[*To* PIPER, *throwing down a brown envelope*] There's your pay packet, Piper. Fifty quid, just like you said.
Piper	[*Picking it up*] I'll take it cos I need it. But you'll be sorry.
Baron	You scratchpenny, patchbacked slinkfoot!
Mayoress	You mudgrubbing, fiddletoed stinkeramus!
Baron	You threaten us, do you? Do your worst!
Mayoress	Blow your pipe until you burst!
Baron	Now get out of Hamelin!
Citizens	Out! Out! Out!
Piper	Before I go, may I have permission to sing a song for the children?
Baron	Certainly not.
Egbert	[*Howls*] But I want a little song.
Mayoress	There, there of course.
Baron	All right. But I don't want a troublemaking song.
Piper	You choose what the song's about. Whatever you like. What do you like best in the world?
Baron	Robots. Because they do what they're told. [*To* CITIZENS] It'd be a good thing if you could teach your children to act more like robots.
Piper	Well here's a song about a robot. Toffee, you help me.
	[PIPER *plays* ROBOT *and* TOFFEE *plays* TOFFEE *in following song*]
Piper	Ronnie the Rusty Robot Was chucked on the rubbish dump For he had a dud computer And a faulty lubricant pump [*Indicates heart*] Ronnie the Rusty Robot His system was out of juice And most of his wires were haywire And his memory circuits were loose

Ronnie the Rusty Robot
Called out from his rubbish tip:
Please bring me a drink of Esso
And a tasty silicon chip

Fair's fair
If you don't play fair
You'll lose your friends
So best beware
Fair dos
Let's have fair dos
Not heads you win
And tails I lose

Piper, Toffee and Children

Fair's fair
If you don't play fair
You'll lose your friends
So best beware
Fair dos
Let's have fair dos
Not heads you win
And tails I lose

Toffee

Toffee the Trusty Truant
Cried out: You've got nothing to fear
She said: I will save your sockets
For I'm a great engineer

Toffee produced her toolkit
She checked every bolt and screw
And when she had finished working
Ronnie looked much better than new

Piper

Ronnie did not say: Thank you,
I'm happy to know you chum.
He drew back a metal welly
And kicked his friend up the bum.

Toffee

Toffee, when she recovered,
She fought back with lots of heart
She bust him in little pieces
She took that robot apart

Then she fed all the pieces
To ostriches in the Zoo, sir
And when they came out the other end
They looked much better than you, sir.

Piper, Toffee and Children
> Fair's fair
> If you don't play fair
> You're going to be
> A mincemeat Mayor
> Fair dos
> A thousand quid
> Or you'll end up
> Like Ronnie did
>
> Fair's fair
> If you don't play fair
> You're going to be
> A mincemeat Mayor
> Fair dos
> A thousand quid
> Or you'll end up
> Like Ronnie did
> Like Ronnie the Rusty Robot did!

Baron   Boggle! Goggle! This scragbeetle has gone off his dip. Throw him in the rubbish cart.

[BOGGLE *and* GOGGLE *pick up the* PIPER]

Toffee   Leave him alone, you bullies.

Mayoress   And while you're about it throw that cabbagesniffer [*Indicating* TOFFEE] in the cart as well. Children, go back to your homes!

[BOGGLE *and* GOGGLE *throw* PIPER *and* TOFFEE *into the rubbish truck. Awful sound of metal and breaking glass as they land out of sight – on a mattress of course.* BARON *rubs his hands. A good day's work.* ADULT CITIZENS *march off with* BARON *and* MAYORESS *singing, as* CHILDREN *follow them reluctantly, singing the Fair's fair chorus half under their breaths.* MAYORESS *drags* EGBERT *away. The heads of the* PIPER *and* TOFFEE *appear over the edge of the truck*]

Piper   You all right, Toffee?

Toffee   I got banged on me nut.

Piper   I'll play it a tune to make it better.

[PIPER *plays his pipe next to* TOFFEE*'s head. She smiles*]

Toffee   Better already . . . you know, I'm a bit sorry for those old rats, drowning to death in that lonely water.

Piper	Those rats was covered with the germs of the dreaded purple plague. You'd have felt <u>really</u> sorry if you came out in purple bumps.
Toffee	They should have paid you.
Piper	Rats got no money.
Toffee	No, I mean the Baron and his friends.
Piper	I'd have done the job for nothing. But he did promise.
Toffee	How did you manage it?
Piper	Manage what?
Toffee	Manage to get those old rats into the river.
Piper	Promise not to tell.
Toffee	I've got nobody I could tell, have I?
Piper	Except me.
Toffee	Well, I promise not to tell you.
Piper	Listen careful, I'll tell you the secret. You know some people study foreign languages till they can talk them like foreigners? Like French [*Demonstrates*] or Italian [*Demonstrates*] or very posh English [*Demonstrates*]
Toffee	Yes.
Piper	Well, I spent years studying rat language. Like, when two rats are having a fight they go [*He gives a series of whistles as if calling a dog*] Then, when one's been beat and he wants to say Pax, he lies on his back and goes [*He gives a long level Swannee whistle which goes neither up nor down*] And when they're courting, which is mostly, because your rat is a very romantic creature, they go like this [*Series of whistles which sound like Louis Louis Louuuuuu, Louis Louis Louis Louis Louuuuuu*] Anyway, the squeaks they make is higher than my mouth can whistle – but this pipe can play notes so high that only rats and bats can hear them. So all I has to do is play a pack of rats the tune that means: Dinner's ready – and they'll follow me through fire and Fulham.
Toffee	That's magic.
Piper	That's music. Every creature uses it. Even earthworms sing to each other. And the sparrows have their mystery dances.
Toffee	What are we going to do, Piper? I've lost my job and you've been cheated rotten.

Piper	Let's have a sulk. I feel right sulky.
Toffee	Sulking's babyish.
Piper	Don't care. I feel like a good old sulk.
Toffee	All right. We'll both sulk.

[PIPER *and* TOFFEE *settle down to a good old sulk. They don't notice that behind and around them* EGBERT *and the* CHILDREN *are arriving, still wearing their school cloaks*]

Egbert   Piper? Are you all right? We've come to cheer you up.

[PIPER *goes into his Patchwork Rap. During this,* EGBERT *and the* CHILDREN *reverse their cloaks so that they now hang behind their shoulders almost like wings. On the reverse of the boring school cloaks are wonderful patchwork patterns, each one different from the other. Some* CHILDREN *perform solo dances – break-dancing etc. By the end of the rap, all of the* CHILDREN *are in patchwork cloaks*]

Piper   I'm a touch lazy
Don't like doing much work
But I often get the itch
To pitch into some patchwork
It may be a hotchpotch
Like fretwork or such work
When I slouch on my couch
And I fetch out my patchwork

First I snatch a patch
From the batch in my pouch
But the patch doesn't match
The patches on my patchwork
So I catch another patch
From the batch in my satchel
And this one matches
The patches on my patchwork.
So I take my patch
And attach it with stitches
Patch against patch
Where the patchwork matches
But if it doesn't match
Even after it's attached
Then the mismatched stitch
Has to be detached . . .

[*Percussion break*]

Piper   You know.

Toffee and Children
               What?

Piper
               I don't like thatchwork
Don't like ditchwork
Only kind I favour
Is my patchwork stitchwork
And soon my patchwork's
Going like clockwork
Sharper than a pitchfork
Neater than brickwork
Hotter than a firework
Cooler than a waxwork.

Piper and Toffee So I snatch a patch
From the batch in my pouch
But the patch doesn't match
The patches on my patchwork
So I catch another patch
From the batch in my satchel
And this one matches
The patches on my patchwork.
So I take my patch
And attach it with stitches
Patch against patch
Where the patchwork matches
And I keep on patching
Till everything's matching
And I keep on stitching
Till I've filled up the kitchen
With my rich rich rich rich
Wider than a soccer pitch
Wonderful colourful patchwork quilt!

Toffee
               Yeah, now what?

Piper
               We're all going on a journey.

Toffee
               Where are we going to?

Piper
               All the way to Koppelburg Mountain.

Toffee
               How do we get there?

Piper
               Over the Shivering Bridge of Dilvergibbon
Where the river down below is like a silver ribbon
But you mustn't look down or your head will turn round

Toffee	I mustn't look down or my head will turn round What'll we do when we reach the mountain?
Piper	We'll do whatever we have to do Bring yourself if you're coming too.

[PIPER *begins to play a strange melody, which develops a strong rhythm*]

[CHILDREN, *including* EGBERT *begin to follow the* PIPER *in a stomping, spiralling dance around the stage*]

[PIPER *leads the* CHILDREN *with* TOFFEE *up the side aisle of the theatre, out of the auditorium, and back down the centre aisle*]

[*A rickety looking bridge is ahead of them, leading from the stalls on to the stage*]

Scene Two

[*The Shivering Bridge of Dilvergibbon.* CHILDREN *pour down the aisle towards the Bridge.* PIPER *and* TOFFEE *encourage them to cross*]

Piper	Right. Easy does it. Over the Shivering Bridge of Dilvergibbon Where the river down below is like a silver ribbon.
Toffee	Don't look down or your head will turn round.
Piper	It's only a drop of about two miles. Don't look down or your head will turn round.

[PIPER *asks audience to join in this chant. Eventually all* CHILDREN *have crossed*]

Good work, my friends, now –

[EGBERT *appears at the far side of the bridge*]

Egbert	Hello! Hello!
Piper	Who's that?
Toffee	It's Egbert!
Egbert	Where are you off to?
Toffee	To the Mountain.
Egbert	Can I come too? I've brought my Australian telly so we can watch "Neighbours".

[EGBERT *holds aloft a trick wooden* TV *set with a strange T-shaped handle on top and no screen. It is a magician's trick with a box within the outer box so that, when worn on the head, it can give the illusion that the wearer's head is being revolved, in either direction*]

Piper   Of course you can come to the Mountain.

Egbert   Yarang! [*Dances for joy, then starts to cross Bridge*] Sounds like a monster roaring down there. [EGBERT *starts to lean over the bridge*]

Toffee   Look out!

Piper   Look up!

[*Too late.* EGBERT *has looked down and his head is twisting itself round. He manages to stagger to the far side of the Bridge*]

Egbert   Me poor old napper! It's twisting itself round. Hellup! Hellup!

Piper   Quick! Put your Australian telly on your head. [*This is accomplished*] We'll soon have your nut untwisted.

[*Twisting business*]

Egbert   Too far! Twist me head back! [*Headturner reversed*] Phew! That's better. [*Headturner taken off*] Thanks a lot. Which way do we go now?

Toffee   The earth's a bit boggy.

Piper   Don't worry. I've got a magic map. [*Produces it. Magic Map has lips and appears to whisper to* PIPER] It says we're about to enter the Bottomless Swamp of Ombroglio.

[*Lights up an area which contains a strange kind of bushy thing apparently covered with hand-shaped fruits*]

[TOFFEE *points to the apparent bush*]

Toffee   What's that – thing? I'm dead sure it moved.

Piper   Nothing to worry about, Toffee, that's the well-known Ombroglio bush festooned with delightful and disgusting Ombroglio fruits.

Egbert   Uh uh! I've just looked it up in my Monster Book of Monsters and it's the Rampant Umbrage – a hairy monster with uncountable hands!

Piper, Toffee and Children
                 A monster? [*All scared*]

[MONSTER *starts to move towards them. All cower save* EGBERT]

Egbert   Hello, Rampant Umbrage. I'm Egbert. May I shake hands with you?

Monster   My pleasure. My pleasure. My pleasure.

                [*They do a handshake routine while the others regain their nerve and join in the handshaking*]

Toffee   We're on our way to the mountain. Can you tell us how to get safely over the Bottomless Swamp?

Monster   You must stomp in the swamp
                To find the ground that's sound.
                That's how Umbrages
                Travel around.
                Carry on along that way and you'll soon come to the Freezing Forest of Forafter.

Egbert   Thank you, Rampant Umbrage. I'll tick you off in my monster spotting book. You're the best monster I've ever seen.

Monster   Thank you. Can I come with you to the mountain?

Piper   You don't eat children, do you?

Monster   Not without tomato sauce.

Piper   Come along then.

Monster   Now remember:
                You must stomp in the swamp
                To find the ground that's sound.
                That's how Umbrages
                Travel around.

All   Stomp in the swamp
                To find the ground that's sound.
                That's how Umbrages
                Travel around.

                [*They do so and proceed on their way*]

                [*Snow begins to fall*]

                [PIPER, TOFFEE, EGBERT *and* CHILDREN *trudging on the spot through the snow*]

                [*Blue lights up on the* ADULTS OF HAMELIN *including the* BARON *and* MAYORESS *staring disconsolately out into the* AUDIENCE. *They sing*]

Adults of Hamelin

> Where have our children gone?
> Where have our children gone?
> Lost in the forest
> Or drowned in the ditches?
> Eaten by lions
> Or stolen by witches?
> Gone missing, gone missing, gone missing.
>
> Where have our children gone?
> Where have our children gone?
> Captured by giants
> Or buried in blizzards?
> Swallowed for breakfast
> By man-eating lizards?
> Gone missing, gone missing, gone missing.
>
> Where have our children gone?
> Where have our children gone?
> Bitten by vampires
> Or flattened by tractors?
> Sunk in a swamp or
> Run off to be actors?
> Gone missing, gone missing, gone missing.
>
> [*This is slow, sad and bewildered*]
>
> [PIPER *and* PARTY *arrive through the snow at the Frozen Forest –
> represented by at least five silver birch trees apparently frozen
> during a high wind and one high silver birch stump*]

Egbert   [*Looking at map*] This must be the Freezing Forest of Forafter.

Piper   The Magic Map says:
                  If you're freezing in the frosts
                  Of the Forest of Forafter
                  Wave your branches in the air
                  And shudder with laughter.

                  [ALL *try this exercise, but soon run out of steam*]

Toffee   Doesn't seem to be working. I've got icicles in my earholes.

Egbert   I think my toes have froze.

Children   We're all going to freeze to death! [*Mass shivering*]

Monster   Look! A knight in armour. We're saved!

[*Lights up on a knight in armour with an axe covered in icicles.* KNIGHT *stands among trees. There is a tree-stump nearby*]

Piper   No good. It's an iced knight.

Egbert   Frozen solid.

Toffee   What can we do?

Child   Why not blow on the knight in armour and melt the ice?

Piper, Toffee, and Egbert
              Great idea!

              [*All gather round and blow on the* KNIGHT]

Piper   Not enough blow-power. [*To* AUDIENCE] Will you help?

              [AUDIENCE *blows.* KNIGHT *begins to move*]

              That's it! Stop blowing!

              [KNIGHT *raises axe and begins to walk slowly towards the travellers. They back away hastily*]

              Gallant Knight, can you save us? We're being deep frozen by this frosty forest.

              [KNIGHT *pushes back helmet.* KNIGHT *is a woman*]

Knight   By the crumbs of Christmas, you need a fire.

Toffee   But we've got nothing to burn.

Knight   Then I'll chop you some dead wood, by the beetles of Birmingham.

              [KNIGHT *smites tree-stump, which immediately falls into neat discs of wood with which* TOFFEE *and* EGBERT *lay a fire which instantly glows. All the travellers including* KNIGHT *sit around, warming their hands*]

Knight   Thank you for melting me. They call me the Iced Knight. [*To* PIPER] But who are you?

Toffee   His name's a secret.

Knight   Where are you bound?

Piper   We're on our way to Koppelburg Mountain.

Knight   Why go there?

Toffee   We don't really know. We're following the Piper.

Piper   Reason we're going is to find a secret country. Where we can be happy.

Toffee   What's it like?

Piper   [CHILDREN *join in the last two lines of each verse*]
                     There is no money
                     So there's no crime
                     There are no watches
                     Cos there's no time
                     It's a good country
                     It's a secret country
                     And it's your country and mine

                     If something's needed
                     You make it there
                     And we have plenty
                     For we all share
                     It's a kind country
                     It's a secret country
                     And it's your country and mine

                     There are no cages
                     There is no zoo
                     But the free creatures
                     Come and walk with you
                     It's a strange country
                     It's a secret country
                     And it's your country and mine

                     There are no prisons
                     There are no poor
                     There are no weapons
                     There is no war
                     It's a safe country
                     It's a secret country
                     And it's your country and mine

                     And in that country
                     Grows a great tree
                     And it's called Freedom
                     And its fruit is free
                     In that blue country
                     In that loving countrty
                     In that wild country
                     In that secret country
                     Which is your country and mine

Piper and Children

> And in that country
> Grows a great tree
> And it's called Freedom
> And its fruit is free
> In that blue country
> In that warm country
> In that loving country
> In that wild country
> In that secret country
> Which is your country and mine.

Piper   Iced Knight of the Frozen Forest, would you like to come with us?

Knight   I would, by the Plughole of Pluto, but I have an urgent quest I must pursue. I seek my brother, who was placed under a spell by a wicked wurzel of a wizard.

Toffee   What was the spell?

Knight   He was changed into a monster!

Egbert   What sort of monster, I've got a book about monsters and –

Knight   A very rare monster called the Rampant Umbrage. Oh, but now I'll never find him.

Monster   That's me. I never recognised you in that sardine outfit.

Knight   By the hairy hobgoblins of Hamelin.

Monster   [*Sings*]
               Alison!

Knight   [*Sings*]
               Humphrey!

Monster   [*Sings*]
               My sister!

Knight   [*Sings*]
               My brother!

Knight and Monster

> [*Sing*]
> We're reunited now
> With one another

Monster   Alison! It's been seven years, seven days and seven hours.

Knight	Humphrey! He turned you into a hairy monster with uncountable hands! But we'll find the spell which will turn you back into a man.
Monster	Why bother with that?
Knight	So that you can go back to your old job as headmaster of a primary school.
Monster	[*Scratches head*] No thanks, I'd sooner be a hairy monster with uncountable hands.
Knight	Good thinking, by the million moons of Mulligatawny.

[*We begin to see the Mountain*]

Piper	Come along you two. It's time to go to the Mountain. Toffee, will you put out the fire?

[*The* PIPER, *playing his pipe softly, leads the* CHILDREN, *the* MONSTER *and the* KNIGHT *towards the Mountain*]

[TOFFEE *is way behind. The* PIPER *notices*]

Piper	We've got to hurry. Egbert, run back and tell Toffee.
Egbert	We've got to hurry up, Toffee.
Toffee	Just a moment, Egbert.
Egbert	Are you all right? [*Toffee nods*] You know, I thought I'd be homesick. But the journey's so exciting that I don't feel sick at all. I could give you a piggyback. My mum doesn't think I'm strong, but I am truly. And with you being a cripple –
Toffee	Don't call me a cripple!
Egbert	What am I supposed to call you?
Toffee	Toffee. Just Toffee. That's my name. I don't want people to think of me as that cripple, or that schoolkid, or that white girl, or that servant. I want people to think of me as Toffee Jenkins. Because I am Toffee Jenkins and I'm special and I'll use my own two legs, the good one and the bad one, to get myself to the Mountain. You run ahead. Tell the Piper Toffee's on her way.
Egbert	But if you do need help, Toffee –
Toffee	[*Smiling*] If I do need help – I'll shout. Thanks Egbert. [EGBERT *runs ahead and joins the* PIPER]

Egbert	Toffee's all right. She doesn't want any help.
Piper	Good. Come on. Soon the Mountain will open its door for a few moments. And when it does, we'll all run, fast as ferrets, into the Mountain. And there we'll find our secret country.

[*Music and a rumbling sound*]

[*The door in the Mountain opens*]

[*The* PIPER, *playing his pipe, runs in with* EGBERT, MONSTER, KNIGHT & CHILDREN. PIPER *turns and places his pipe outside the Mountain*]

Toffee	Wait!

[*She stumbles. The door of the Mountain closes*]

Toffee	Piper!

[*There is a shouting. The* BARON, MAYORESS *and* CITIZENS *appear and stare at* TOFFEE]

Arianalla	Where are our children?
Toffee	They're all gone.
Cosima	Won't we ever get them back?
Toffee	Oh no, no. But you might be able to see them. If everyone helps me sing. [*To* AUDIENCE] If I sing you a line of a song, will you sing it back to me?

[TOFFEE, CITIZENS *and* AUDIENCE *sing in order to make the Mountain open and show the children*]

[*A slow, magical, melodious song, maybe with echoes and a throbbing rhythm underneath*]

Koppelburg
Koppelburg
Koppelburg hillside
Open your
Windows and
Show us your inside.

Koppelburg
Koppelburg
Koppelburg mountain
Open your
Windows and
Show us the children.

[*The song, taught and conducted by* TOFFEE, *should be sung
by more and more of the* AUDIENCE, *building from very quiet
to a cumulative climax upon which the mountain becomes
transparent, translucent and we can see the* CHILDREN *and the* PIPER
and the MONSTER *and* KNIGHT]

Toffee   [*Sings*]
Inside the mountain the children are happy as acrobats
    tumbling down fields of clover
Nobody's punished and everyone's gentle and wild as a
    waterfall's water
Sitting in rivers each day of the summer and igloos and furs in
    winter
Islands and antelopes, tulips and unicorns singing in out-of-
    door theatres
Jumping down sand-dunes and cloud-mountaineering and
    learning the language of fishes
Building new fountains and under-earth diving and sharing
    your daydreams and swapping your whispers.

And freedom's the music
And peace is the dance
And love is the weather
And love is the flower

And there is no money
And there is no hurting
And there is no screaming
And there is no power

Toffee and Children
For freedom's the music
And peace is the dancing
And love is the making
And love is the breathing
And love is the mountain
Inside the mountain
Inside the mountain of
Love.

Toffee   [*To* AUDIENCE] Did you see the children?

[*The* BARON, MAYORESS *and* CITIZENS *turn their backs on* TOFFEE *and the
Mountain*]

Baron   It's just a mountain. I can't see anything in it.

Mayoress   Of course not. The child's talking nonsense.

Doctor   I think there must be a moral to this story. But what is it?

Baron, Mayoress and Citizens

[*Sing*]

An apple a day will gather no moss
A new broom spoils the pot
Don't count your bridges before they hatch
Strike while the chicken is hot
If you're over the parrot now
You're going to be sick as a moon
You've got to pay the piper
If the piper plays your tune.

A gander in time keeps the doctor away
And look before you lake
All that is Gary is glittering
Burn your Ignorance Cake
If you're over the parrot now
You're going to be sick as a moon
You've got to pay the piper
If the piper plays your tune.

There's too many cooks in houses of glass
You're better safe than dead
Put all your acorns in one goose
Eggs are worth two in the head
If you're over the parrot now
You're going to be sick as a moon
You've got to pay the piper
If the Piper plays your tune.

[*We can still see inside the mountain*]

Toffee

Inside the mountain they're happy as hampers as daft as old dolphins at sea.
Zebras lie down with them, elephants walk with them, everywhere, everywhere

Meadows like trampolines, horses like Pegasus, silver rats telling them jokes.
Edward Lear lives with them, John Lennon sings for them, any old day of the week.

Nobody's crippled and nobody's troubled and nobody's ever afraid.
Fish and chip hedges by vinegar ditches and shining cheeseburger trees.

Toffee, Piper, Egbert, Monster, Knight and Children

For freedom's the music
And peace is the dancing

And love is the making
And love is the breathing
Inside the mountain
Inside the mountain
Inside the mountain of love.

And freedom's the music
And peace is the dance
And love is the weather
And love is the flower
Inside the mountain

And there is no money
And there is no hurting
And there is no screaming
And there is no power . . .

[*During the song the* CHILDREN *in the Mountain sing some nonsense chord words to provide musical punctuation*]

Children   Nolleyfizz . . . Jumblein . . . Paddleboot . . . Holleybeem . . .
Roodle-aid . . . Dunnywam . . . Onnygong . . . Glabberdum . . .

[*Eventually the song in the Mountain and the song of the* CITIZENS *are simultaneous, the* CHILDREN *singing about their happiness, the* ADULTS *pointing out a lot of weird morals*]

[TOFFEE *turns and walks back to the Mountain. It remains closed.* TOFFEE *squats and picks up something. She stands and turns and we see she carries the* PIPER*'s pipe*]

Toffee   The Piper must have left it. There's some scratches on the
pipe. Words.
"For Toffee with love – from Peter Bunting." That must have
been his secret name. Peter Bunting.

[TOFFEE *smiles*]

Toffee   [*Sings*]
One day soon I'm going to spread my wings and fly away,
Fly away.

[*She walks down the stage. She lifts the pipe and begins to play*]

[*She walks through the* AUDIENCE *and away. A shooting star whizzes across the sky*]

[*We hear it. It makes a fizzing sound*]

The End

The Pied Piper

A cassette recording of music by Dominic Muldowney from the Royal National Theatre's production of 'The Pied Piper' is on sale in the Royal National Theatre Bookshop at £2.99

It is also available by post from: the Bookshop, Royal National Theatre, South Bank, London SE1 9PX
Please add 85p for postage and packing

Songs included on the tape are:

Hamelin Town *Full Company*
River Water *Diane Bull* (Toffee Jenkins)
Pestilential Parasites *Sylvester McCoy* (Pied Piper)
Gorgonzola Moon *Brian Hibbard* (King Rat)
Good Riddance *Full Company*
Secret Country *Sylvester McCoy* (Pied Piper)
Ronnie the Rusty Robot *Sylvester McCoy and Diane Bull*
Koppelburg Mountain *Diane Bull*
Inside the Mountain *Diane Bull and Company*

Pied Piper Company
Mary Askham, Allister Bain, Diane Bull, Jimmy Chisholm, Brian Hibbard, Sylvester McCoy, Philip McGough, Bill Moody, Bruce Purchase, Patsy Rowlands, Ewart James Walters, Doreen Webster with the children from Dog Kennel Hill Junior School, East Dulwich, London.

Musicians
Robert Lockhart *(MD/keyboards)*, Julia Findon *(trumpet)*, Michael Gregory *(drums)*, David Stewart *(trombone)*, David Roach *(saxophone/electronic wind instruments)*.